Chakras

Discover How Your Chakras Benefit You And How To Use
Them As A Guide In Your Daily Life

*(An Easy-to-use Guide To Chakra Meditation Techniques
For Opening, Balancing, And Purifying)*

Eduardo Beltran

TABLE OF CONTENT

Introduction 1

Balancing Chakras 4

Solar Plexus Chakra Imbalance Outward Manifestations 26

Utilizing Stones And Crystals 40

How To Maintain Your Stones Or Crystals 55

Guided Meditation 79

System Of Nutrition And Chakras 94

Other Methods For Caring For The Chakras . 103

The Sources Of Chakra Information 114

Introduction

According to modern scientific theories, the universe had a finite beginning in the "Big Bang." From a scientific standpoint, it is believed that an infinitesimally small yet unfathomably dense molecule randomly erupted all of creation into existence during this event that is still difficult to comprehend. All matter that has ever existed or ever will exist was contained in a subatomic structure smaller than this period. Me, you, the Earth, the sun, and the moon, as well as entire galaxies, were all compressed into something too tiny to be seen without a microscope.

According to ancient Indian philosophers, this was true thousands of years before NASA considered the possibility. According to the beliefs underlying the concept of chakra, we are all fundamentally one being, deriving from the same source but manifesting in various forms. The human, the tree, and the rock are all manifestations of the same cosmic energy field. We experience individuality and a sense of separation only when this energy is harnessed within one of these physical constructs.

Imagine a table strewn with a variety of vessels, each with a unique form and construction. Now, distribute one gallon of water equitably among the containers. There are tall, short, slender, and wide receptacles. They appear different on the outside, but they contain the same water from the same source. According to the foundations of a belief in the chakra system, as humans, we are identical to those vessels; the same cosmic water travels through all of us; it has simply been emptied into a diverse array of containers.

It is the experience of perception mediated through the five senses of the human body that generates the strong emotions of separation we experience as distinct beings operating in this reality. Similar to the various containers containing the same water, we believe that we are inherently unique and distinct from others. For most, it is only upon mortality and separation from the physical form that we become aware of our true, eternal essence.

But even in the absence of these divine revelations, acute disconnection from the same cosmic, universal lifeforce can cause problems in this life. We are unable to pinpoint it, but there is a vacancy that needs to be filled. Although we are separated in various vessels of flesh and blood, we still yearn for a sense of unity and completeness. The restorative properties of the chakras aim to direct you in this direction. Read on to find out how.

Balancing Chakras

When someone discusses harmonizing the chakras, they are referring to a variety of concepts and methods. A straightforward definition of chakra balancing is the process of restoring the chakra's energy to a state of harmony and optimal function.

Chakra balancing is only a portion of the whole picture. Each chakra in the system must be able to operate as a unit. If we take the time to examine how chakras function, we can observe that they have a force that connects them and that they interact energetically. When balancing our chakras, it is crucial to consider not only each chakra in isolation, but also their neighboring energy centers and the energy that circulates throughout the entire system.

7 Indicators That Your Chakras Are Imbalanced

Weight Problems

The affected chakras will be the sacral chakra, solar plexus chakra, and root chakras. Most people believe that lifestyle, diet, and behavior, in addition to exercise, are the primary causes of weight concerns; however, most do not consider lack of grounding to be a cause. If we do not feel grounded, the root chakra is malfunctioning. If the root chakra is in harmony, we will sense a strong connection to nature. No matter what challenges we face in life, knowing that our fundamental needs are met makes us feel safe. The majority of us gain weight to feel more grounded.

We may use weight as a buffer between ourselves and the world when our self-esteem is low or when we feel intimidated or assaulted. Consequently, our solar plexus chakra may be out of balance. The solar plexus chakra represents our power center. It aids in confidence, self-worth, and self-control.

Occasionally, we have difficulty experiencing joy and connecting with our emotions. If we do not process the emotions that may have influenced our sentiments of survival and self-worth, we will not feel pleasure when we consume and our sacral chakra will become unbalanced.

Anorexia may have been diagnosed if you have a severe problem with low body weight, an intense dread of acquiring any weight, and a distorted perception of your weight. People with anorexia severely restrict the amount of food they consume. Bulimia occurs when a person consumes a large quantity of food and then either takes a laxative, induces vomiting, or engages in excessive exercise. Both of these disorders result in harsh evaluations of a person's appearance, as sufferers believe they must be extremely slender to be respectable. Because they believe they have physical defects, individuals may have difficulty regulating their self-image. Both of these conditions are the result of an imbalanced solar plexus.

Mental Disorders

All chakras can be affected by anxiety. It depends entirely on the sort of anxiety being experienced. Anxiety is an everyday occurrence. When an intense, persistent, or excessive fear dominates our lives, it is completely incapacitating. If you suffer from anxiety, it could quickly transform into despair or dread, resulting in a panic attack. It can also diminish the quality of our lives.

It depends on the type of anxiety you experience, but it could affect any of the involved chakras. If the crown chakra is out of alignment, we may feel disconnected from God, Goddess, the Universe, the Source, or the Divine. If our apprehension is caused by the third eye being out of equilibrium, we fear the unknown and have little faith in our intuition. If your vocal chakra is unbalanced, you may experience anxiety when expressing your emotions, expressing yourself, and communicating with others. Your solar plexus chakra is out of balance if you feel intimidated, under pressure to perform well, entirely inundated by everything, or entangled in a power struggle within a relationship. If your sacral chakra is out of balance, you will experience feelings of remorse or guilt because you have not fully processed your intense emotions. This can occur as a result of past traumas such as sexual assault. The root chakra is unbalanced if we worry about our ability to survive in this world, such as money, shelter, and sustenance. This makes us feel like we are in a constant state of survival.

The chakras afflicted by depression are the heart and crown chakras. Depression has numerous causes. Occasionally, it may travel through temporarily. At other times, it may be an everlasting presence in our existence. Depression could be incapacitating for those who suffer from it. Depression may be experienced as a persistent sense of futility, desolation, or sorrow. You may not enjoy your daily activities and believe that life is not worth living. It may interfere with your sleep or appetite, causing you to slumber excessively or not at all. You may have even considered suicide or mortality.

When melancholy, you will experience a profound sense of isolation. Crown chakra is balanced and open when you feel connected to the world and the universe. If you experience resentment toward the Universe regarding your existence, this indicates that your energy is out of balance. Depression may result from an unbalanced heart chakra because we are not connected to ourselves.

The chakras affected by panic attacks are the root, solar plexus, and heart chakras. The onset of a panic attack is marked by incapacitating, acute, and sudden anxiety. These symptoms may be accompanied by feelings of impending catastrophe, shortness of breath, shivering, trembling, perspiration, an elevated pulse rate, a throbbing heart, and palpitations. If we are not connected to our heart chakra and do not heed to what it is telling us, these attacks are possible. When fear and hysteria set in, the root chakra is activated because our concern for survival is triggered. Since confidence and self-esteem reside in the solar plexus, if the heart chakra feels disconnected and we are in a constant state of dread, the solar plexus feels as if it has been struck in the stomach.

Cancer

This dreadful disease affects each and every chakra. Cancer develops when abnormal cells proliferate at an uncontrollable rate. They invade and destroy healthy tissue. This can occur on multiple levels, and symptoms can vary depending on the affected body part. Symptoms may include thickened areas beneath the skin, palpable tumors, skin changes, weight fluctuations, and fatigue, among others. The environment, health conditions, family history, practices, and age can all increase the likelihood of developing cancer. According to the Mayo Clinic, the majority of malignancies occur in individuals with no known risk factors. Cancer may be the result of unprocessed, denied, or neglected profound pain and resentment. It can manifest as noxious emotions, such as sorrow or loathing, that consume us.

These manifest on multiple levels as a result of an imbalance in particular chakras:

Esophageal, laryngeal, and thyroid cancers: Throat chakra

Heart and pharynx chakras and lung cancer

Cancer of the brain: Crown chakra

Root and sacral chakras and prostate and rectal cancer

Sacral chakra and cancers of the rectum, colon, uterus, ovaries, and cervix

Pancreatic, intestinal, liver, and stomach cancers: Solar plexus chakra

Heart chakra: Breast cancer

Headaches

The crown and third-eye chakras are affected by this. If you experience migraines that are not the result of physical imbalances, it may be a sign that one of your chakras is out of whack. If you have a frontal headache accompanied by symptoms of pressure behind the eyes or cranial pressure, this is typically a sign of discord in the third eye.

This form of discomfort could be a sign that you have been concentrating on your intellect and are afraid of your spirituality. You can only see actuality, and you have no faith in your intuition. When you experience these symptoms, it is because you disregard your own inner knowledge. If you receive "hints" but do not act on them, you are not respecting the wisdom of your third eye. You may feel the need to seek out new opportunities, but you do not. You may also experience knowing that a particular person is unwell and will not want to be around others. You engage them regardless. Intuitive cues that contradict one another may cause discord and imbalance in the third eye chakra.

If you have a discomfort in the center of the top of your skull, it may be due to an imbalance in the crown chakra. This could indicate that you have difficulty trusting your life path, seeing the bigger picture, or having faith in yourself and your connection to the Divine. You may also feel unfulfilled or lonely.

Reproductive Issues

The solar plexus, root, and sacral chakras are all affected by infertility. Infertility is the inability of a woman to conceive after multiple attempts and more than a year. Infertility is a common occurrence, but the woman's dread and anguish can cause a great deal of stress and even humiliation. The sacral chakra is affected because it is associated with the genitalia and placenta and is the emotional center of the body. Most individuals who struggle with infertility experience a variety of intense emotions. It causes them to question, "Am I making the correct choice?"Do I even desire to become a parent?"Do I have the appropriate partner?"I may not even be a good parent." "How will this affect my life?""

There could be physical causes such as a high level of follicle-stimulating hormone, absence of menstruation, low sperm count, or poor egg quality. There is typically a high level of tension among couples who are attempting to conceive. As infertility can cause family problems, the root chakra is also implicated. Individuals who are attempting to conceive without the support of a significant other may experience additional difficulty. They may also be concerned about carrying on negative characteristics to their offspring. Making a new existence is a challenge to a person's self-esteem; it can make them feel impotent, which is a problem for the solar plexus, our power center.

The sacral chakra is impacted by uterine cysts and fibroid tumors. According to the Mayo Clinic, uterine fibroids are noncancerous growths within the uterus. They frequently occur during the reproductive years. Numerous women may develop uterine fibroids at some point in their lifetimes. Most of the time, they do not produce symptoms, but in some cases, they can develop to a large size and cause discomfort during menstruation, digestive movements, and digestion. They can cause respiratory difficulties.

Cysts are fluid-filled sacs that are found on the ovaries. If there is a growth within the uterus, this may indicate an imbalance in the sacral chakra. There is a physical obstruction in the reproductive area. The energy indicates that there is an internal energy blockage. You may be holding on to old, noxious, negative thoughts, feelings, or emotions that are attempting to channel energy into dead ends. This could include relationships or professions that you have transcended, as well as those that are incompatible with your relationships, reproduction, abundance, or creativity.

Joint Pain

Hip Pain: If you have problems with your hips that are not caused by physical trauma, the sacral chakra is likely to be the cause. Our hips store a great deal of unprocessed, repressed emotions that we avoid confronting. Since the sacral chakra is the seat of our emotions, if we disregard them we may cause an imbalance.

Leg Pain: The affected chakras are the solar plexus and root chakras. Usually, leg discomfort is caused by an imbalance in the root chakra. Pain in the legs may represent resistance to advancing forward in life. This may manifest as fear-based self-sabotaging behaviors, such as a dread of failure or a fear that we may not achieve our goals. If so, the root chakra may be connected to the solar plexus chakra, and both may be out of balance. It is primarily a root chakra issue as a result of anxiety regarding apparel, water, food, shelter, or expenses.

In this case, the pharynx chakra is afflicted by neck pain. If the neck pain is not the result of a physical injury, it may be that your throat chakra is out of equilibrium as a result of your interactions with the outside world. The pharynx chakra can become unbalanced if you do not express yourself honestly and openly, or if you attempt to conceal specific aspects of yourself, such as insecurities or fears, from others. There are numerous causes for holding yourself back, but the end result is always neck discomfort.

The sacral and root chakras are the chakras afflicted by sciatica. Sciatica is characterized by discomfort that radiates from the lower back through the pelvis, buttocks, and each leg. In the absence of trauma, sciatic pain may indicate an imbalanced root chakra. This chakra is concerned with your existence and survival. If you fear that your fundamental needs will be taken away, whether you can provide for your children, how you will pay your expenses, or whether you will be able to feed today, this indicates that your root chakra is out of balance. Sciatica typically represents your anxiety about the future and your finances. Occasionally, sciatic pain may indicate that you do not feel secure.

Back Pain: If you have back pain that is not caused by physical trauma, it may be a sign of the health of your chakras. Pain could range from a mild discomfort that causes back stiffness to a severe, acute pain that restricts your mobility.

The affected chakras in the upper back are the heart and pharynx chakras. If you do not speak the truth or if you experience grief, threats to loving yourself, or difficulties loving others, the tension may manifest as upper back discomfort or tension. You may sense that you are withholding affection, unloved, or unsupported.

Middle Back: The affected chakras are the solar plexus and heart chakras. You may experience discomfort or tension in the centre of your back if you are struggling with love, holding on to prior wounds, having our power challenged, or feeling cherished. This may occur if you become mired in sentiments from the past and become overwhelmed with regret for things you have said or done.

The affected chakras in the lower back are the root and sacral chakras. If you are experiencing difficulty with creative expression, relationships, or abundance, you may experience lower back discomfort and tension. Back pain may result from repressing these emotions or failing to process them, as well as from difficulties in surviving and meeting fundamental requirements.

Asthma and Allergies

The afflicted chakra is the heart chakra. If your airways are constricted and you produce excessive mucus, you may experience shortness of breath, wheezing, and coughing. If you have allergies, your immune system will produce antibodies that identify a harmless allergen as hazardous. Each of these conditions causes difficulties in daily life. Inflammation of your digestive tract, sinuses, airway, or skin may result from a compromised immune system. Additionally, it could cause respiratory distress. Since these are associated with the heart chakra, such responses may indicate that this chakra is out of balance, particularly if you experience issues with compassion, love, sorrow, and mourning.

10 Advantages of Restoring Your Chakras

If your chakras are aligned and balanced, you will experience external and internal benefits. You may also observe effects at home, school, and work, among other locations. If you feel your finest, you will be optimistic and have faith. You will be more productive and have more self-confidence.

Your chakras must be healed periodically, and you must examine your existence to determine if anything is missing. When you know how to recognize an obstructed chakra, you will always be on the lookout for a chakra that may require cleansing so that you can enjoy the best health.

Acceptance of oneself and self-assurance
Self-confidence, self-acceptance, and self-love are the results of having functional chakras. If you have confidence in yourself, expressing yourself and communicating with others will be less difficult.

Self-realization leads to self-acceptance. This is accomplished by maintaining healthy and balanced chakras. If you have self-awareness, you can accept your limitations and strengths, and you will no longer be intimidated by your weaknesses. You can work on them and transform them into an advantage through effort.

Having access to one's innate knowledge
Having healthy and balanced chakras facilitates your connection to a higher being from which you can perceive your inner self. Once you have a complete understanding of yourself, your self-awareness increases, allowing you to comprehend your vulnerabilities and strengths with greater clarity.

An inner wisdom that guides you to live an impactful and meaningful existence is one of your strengths.

Enhanced relationship with your essence

You will have a stronger connection to your Divine Source when you are able to clear your zenith chakra. Once you recognize your Divine Source and are able to establish a strong connection with them, you will be able to communicate with them and surrender all your problems to them, which will bring you serenity.

Your crown chakra is the chakra associated with your spiritual aspect. If it is well-balanced, it could bring you a great deal of spiritual enlightenment.

You will discover that balancing your yin and yang is quite simple. Osho, an Indian spiritual guru, once said, "You will be in the world, but not of it."

Better expression

If your larynx chakra is obstructed, it is difficult to express yourself authentically. Even a single obstructed chakra can impact the transmission of energy to the other chakras, affecting your entire system.

If your chakras are healthy, you will find it simple to express yourself. This will result in improved relationships, increased life satisfaction, self-acceptance, and self-assurance.

Reduces tension and anxiety

When we store negative energy in our bodies, we may experience negative emotions such as melancholy, rage, fear, anxiety, and tension. All of these have negative effects on our health. Visualization and meditation might be used to heal your chakras. This reduces the likelihood of becoming melancholy, apprehensive, or agitated, and helps you decompress and calm.

Weight reduction

Unhealthy chakras can result in negative emotions such as anxiety and diminished self-esteem. In many cases, these negative emotions may result in an unhealthy lifestyle that contributes to obesity and weight gain.

When chakras are healthy and balanced, these emotions are kept at bay and the likelihood of leading an unhealthy existence is diminished. Diverse yoga poses can restore obstructed chakras, allow energy to circulate throughout the body, and aid in weight loss.

Sleep better

When you have obstructed chakras, your body's vitality becomes stagnant. This negative energy can induce sleeplessness. Meditation is the greatest method to repair an obstructed chakra. This is the most effective treatment for insomnia. If you meditate correctly, you will find it simpler to fall slumber and sleep better overall.

Self-realization

Having healthy chakras will increase your awareness of who you are and help you comprehend your true purpose. Once you recognize your reasons for existing, you will be able to shift your focus from things that do not contribute to your or others' lives to those that do. When you know who you are, you will be on the path to experiencing the greatest success in life.

ardor for existence

When you can establish a connection with the spiritual sphere, you can comprehend the true purpose and significance of existence. This will enhance your zeal for life because you have become a person driven by a sense of purpose. In comparison to those who do not know why they are alive, those who do have a strong desire to attain their objectives. It makes you someone with whom others will want to travel and spend time.

Releasing negative energy in positive ways

When your chakras are out of balance, you contain a great deal of negative energy. It does not have to be this way, as restoring your chakra can assist you in purging your negative emotions. Negative energy can manifest as negative emotions including humiliation, remorse, dread, and rage. There cannot be any negative or stagnant energy contained within you if your energy wheels are rotating in harmony. To make space for all the positive energy, it is eliminated.

It does not imply that life becomes simpler. It means that even in the most difficult circumstances, you will not make things more difficult for yourself. To quote an old adage: "It doesn't get simpler. You just get better."

Solar Plexus Chakra Imbalance Outward Manifestations

The term power best describes this Chakra. People with Solar Plexus Chakra imbalances are disempowered in one way or another, and this manifests as either allowing themselves to be bossed around and controlled by others and by life itself, or, on the other hand, attempting to establish their personal power by bossing others around or attempting to control everything. Although they may appear to be polar opposites, both modes of being stem from a place of insecurity and powerlessness.

Some individuals are disempowered with regard to substances, relying excessively on external stimulants for power or energy, and may feel impotent against the temptation to indulge. This is not limited to food, narcotics, alcohol, or caffeine; some individuals require a constant stream of entertainment or social interaction to "feel alive." In proportion to our dependence on external sources of energy, our Solar Plexus Chakra becomes misaligned.

The physical appearance of the stomach, as well as the general relationship to food, stimulants, narcotics, and alcohol, are indicators of imbalances in this Chakra.

Some individuals have almost no interest in food or are excessively restricted in what they are permitted to consume, causing them to be weakened and more easily exhausted. Low caloric intake may indicate that a person is unconsciously isolating herself from her own power out of dread or is seeking power through body control. A weakened, depressed Chakra may indicate a dread of assuming power, an inward retreat, or a fear of standing out. Alternately, a large stomach may indicate an excessive need for power, dominance, or control, or a simple egocentric desire to occupy space.

Excess weight or chronic overindulgence in food generally indicates a malfunction in the third Chakra, as it indicates that the body is not converting food into energy in a balanced manner. On some level, a person who is "always hungry" is not allowing her own power to circulate freely. As a result of an energy obstruction, she feels compelled to absorb more and more from an external source. This is futile, as overeaters typically experience massive energy "crashs." True nourishment can only be obtained from within.

Addictions typically involve an imbalance in the Solar Plexus Chakra, as this is the center from which we seize control of our lives and initiate the necessary changes. The first and second chakras draw us toward sameness, safety, and routine; without a robust third chakra, we cannot reach new levels to liberate ourselves and discover new behavioral patterns. To ascend to the third Chakra is to assume control over your own existence.

Integrating Jupiter's Energy into the Solar Plexus Chakra

At some point in our lives, we ask ourselves, "Who am I? What Is My Objective?"

There is only one method to discover these answers. It will not be found in your college degrees or awards. It is not found in relationships with peers and family. It cannot be found in your job, residence, physical appearance, or bank account.

Jupiter possesses the answers to these queries. The truth of who you are can be found in what brings you pleasure.

Joy is not a trivial matter. The source of your personal strength is happiness. Strengthens you by practicing alignment with your joy and prioritizing joy in your life. If you are perpetually disconnected from happiness, you cannot be genuinely effective at anything in life. You cannot persuade or inspire others if you are emotionally disconnected. Joy is experiencing the connection to your inner being on the most fundamental level and assuming your place in the universe.

To achieve Solar Plexus Chakra balance, you must construct your existence around the energy of Jupiter. For the health of your Solar Plexus Chakra, it is essential that you prioritize activities, people, and circumstances that uplift you. Construct your life on a foundation of genuine fulfillment and purpose, and discard people or activities that deplete your energy or vitality.

This is not the same as submerging one's head in the sand, turning a closed eye to the tribulations of the world, or disregarding valid criticism of oneself or one's work. It is, however, recognizing that we cannot aid others when we are ourselves feeble, emotionally exhausted, or subjecting ourselves to unnecessary emotional suffering. It is essential to respect the energy that is yours to direct and shield it from harmful influences.

When your Solar Plexus Chakra is robust and healthy, you do not feel depleted or weakened by conflict or confrontation, but rather strengthened. When we are firmly anchored in our pleasure, we have a strong sense of purpose. From this position of strength, we appreciate when our vulnerabilities and faults are brought to our attention, as it affords us the chance to correct them and ultimately become even stronger.

When we are profoundly connected to our true will, we are impervious to slander and assaults, because our fortitude of purpose acts as a buffer against them. This is Jupiter's genuine charm. When we are truly aligned with our true will, we know who is aiding us and who is attempting to bring us down out of jealously. We are too occupied creating gorgeous outcomes to be concerned with the latter.

Expression of the Jupiterian archetype through the Solar Plexus induces a protective sense of oneness with a greater power or purpose. When you pursue the activities or causes that provide you with profound satisfaction, you have an unshakable conviction that your life is worth living. You do not feel the need to ask your mother or father, teacher, employer, children, physician, or psychic if what you are doing is "correct." When you are aligned with this profound inner purpose, the pull of happiness is so intense that you know it is at the very essence of your being, even if it requires you to go against the grain and forge your own path.

Solar Plexus Chakra Reference Chart

The 52-day Planetary Season provides us with the greatest opportunity to engage with Jupiter's energy, as the Solar Chakra is more receptive and active. This cosmic schedule affords you abundant opportunity to honor Jupiter within. Bring yourself into balance by consciously cultivating and allowing the elements of the Jupiter archetype to flourish within you: ambition, generosity, enthusiasm, leadership, and spirituality.

These periods are optimal for detoxifying and/or restoring the liver, pancreas, and digestive tract.

Jupiter's hours, days, and season are optimal periods to reflect on the Solar Plexus Chakra-governed areas of your life or to carry out tasks related to these areas.

These periods are ideal for overcoming bad behaviors, making positive changes, pursuing your passion, and being inspired. Jupiter periods are ideal for connecting with these elevating energies if you have a religious or spiritual practice. In addition, they are ideal for listening to motivational speakers, pursuing higher education, and pondering the larger questions of life. Eat healthily, nourish your body, and rejoice in life!

Explore everything associated with your own will, empowerment, happiness, and energy management. During Jupiter's days, hours, and seasons, activities that stimulate growth or advancement in these areas are especially effective.

Solar Plexus Chakra Balancing through Intention, Receptivity, and Vibrational Entrainment

Everything around us vibrates, and everything that vibrates has consciousness. The vibrations emitted by gemstones, colors, essential oils, music, and more can influence our own vibration, allowing our condition to eventually synchronize with theirs. This phenomenon is referred to as 'entrainment' - our vibrations become more coherent and enter a healthier state.

Jupiter Chakra Gemstones

Take a calm, deep breath and align your vibrational frequency with that of your chosen gemstone.

Yellow sapphire stimulates the Solar Plexus Chakra, concentrates the will, and sustains manifesting intentions.

The 'stone of prosperity' resonates with the vibrations of the third Chakra, the willpower center.

Golden topaz increases personal power, creates abundance, and opens the communication channels between your human self and the Divine Will, bringing a joyous comprehension of the role it plays in one's life.

Bumblebee jasper is the antidote for emotional hesitancy and diminished self-esteem. It enhances one's capacity to recognize and capture opportunities by supporting the "gut" sensation aspect of awareness. It indicates the way to one's highest destiny on a spiritual level.

Saturn Chakra Color

Yellow light and all its variations emanate from the Solar Plexus and represent the psychic qualities within the energy field of the chakra. It is the color with the greatest amount of brightness. Yellow is an uplifting and optimistic color. It clears the psyche and heightens consciousness. It is the hue of illumination and the Sacred.

Jupiter Chakra Essential Oils

All emotions are retained in the amygdala, a portion of the limbic system that is closely aligned with the seven Chakras.

Diffuse or position a few droplets of the essential oil in your palms, massage your hands together, cup your hands over your nostrils, and inhale.

Lime purifies on the emotional and physical levels, enables the third Chakra to receive light, and instills the fortitude to face life's challenges.

The wild orange teaches us about generosity and abundance, and it reminds us of what the soul sees: boundless pleasure and wealth.

Cumin regulates individual strength. It reminds us not to allow our ambitions and desire to come at the expense of others, lest we reach the summit alone. On the path to personal accomplishment, it promotes a healthy sense of self-worth and appreciation for others.

Jupiter Chakra Spiritual Tone

It is also possible to accomplish vibrational entrainment from within by chanting sounds and mantras. This practice can realign frequencies, restore Chakra health, and remove Chakra obstructions.

Although there are numerous sounds associated with the Jupiter Chakra, "RAM" is commonly used to activate this energy center. Concentrate on your third Chakra while rhythmically repeating

"RAM" and visualizing the sound stimulating the Chakra's rotation.

You can also use the resonant "A" vowel sound (as in "father") in your writing.

528 Hertz is the frequency of Solfeggio. This frequency eliminates guilt and establishes limits.

Meditation on the Jupiter Chakra and Invocation

Imagine dazzling yellow vibrations emanating from your Solar Plexus Chakra as you inhale.

Sensitize yourself to the Earth's energy as it rises through you.

Release all feelings of remorse and negative self-talk.

Invoke Jupiter, your personal superpower, to transcend the confines of your current path.

Explore its wealth through the lens of your Soul.

Meditate on the aspects of your life that exemplify faith, pleasure, amusement, zeal, and self-assurance.

Utilizing Stones And Crystals

Crystals are a potent instrument for harmonizing and healing your chakras. Each crystal's healing, balancing, and strengthening of your chakras is facilitated by its unique properties and varied applications.

Each crystal is unique and possesses its own distinct energy, having been formed by natural processes over thousands of years. They can benefit your health in numerous ways, including emotional equilibrium and spiritual enlightenment. In numerous cultures, crystals have been used to aid in the healing of physical maladies, mental and emotional issues, meditation, and spiritual quests since antiquity.

This chapter concentrates on balancing your sacral chakra with crystals and stones. It discusses the properties of various stones and crystals, what makes them beneficial for this chakra, as well as how to use, cleanse, and maintain them.

Crystals' Role in Balancing the Sacral Chakra

In numerous methods, crystals are used for sacral chakra restoration. The purpose of crystals in this healing process is to remove blockages and re-energize the chakra, thereby restoring its optimal equilibrium and function.

There are numerous methods for balancing the sacral chakra with crystals. Utilizing crystals in meditation, transporting them with you, or wearing them are popular techniques. When a crystal is placed directly on the body over the sacral chakra, its energy is able to travel into the chakra and remove any blockages or imbalances.

Here are several methods crystals assist in balancing the sacral chakra:

Restore Balance to the Chakra

Crystals restore the sacral chakra's energetic equilibrium by removing blockages and restoring balance. Carnelian, for example, is a potent sacral chakra stone that enhances motivation and creativity. Citrine is an additional sacral chakra crystal that facilitates positive change by dissolving old patterns and beliefs. By working with sacral chakra crystals, we can release old wounds and obstructions and make room for new levels of creativity, delight, and vitality.

Promote Fertility and Prosperity

People have utilized crystals for their putative magical properties for centuries. Many people still believe that crystals enhance imagination, fecundity, and prosperity. Despite the lack of scientific evidence, some individuals find that working with crystals helps them connect with their creative side. Others use crystals to concentrate their intention on manifesting an abundance of favors in their lives. Others, however, transport crystals to increase their chances of becoming pregnant.

Working with crystals can be an enjoyable and empowering way to connect with your intentions and infuse your life with positive energy, regardless of whether they possess supernatural properties. They are a one-of-a-kind tool for healing and self-discovery, and when used properly, they help raise your vibration, increase your creativity, and attract prosperity.

Releases Traumas and Stress

Stress and trauma are among the most prevalent causes of sacral chakra imbalance. These negative energies have an energy-draining effect, causing us to feel apprehensive, overburdened, and disconnected from our true selves. Using the restorative power of crystals, we can restore balance to our sacral chakra and expel these poisonous energies from our bodies.

Certain crystals, such as jade or aquamarine, have a calming effect on the mind and body, enhancing mindfulness and reducing tension. Other crystals, like amethyst and orange calcite, aid in the discharge of past traumas and negative beliefs that foster anxiety and distress. Therefore, working with crystals is a potent method for healing the sacral chakra for those who wish to reconnect with their authentic sentiments and emotions.

The Distinction Between Rocks and Crystals

Although stones and crystals are frequently used interchangeably, there is a distinction between the two. Natural pebbles that have been shaped or refined are stones. They are available in numerous hues, forms, and sizes. Stones are typically valued for their aesthetic qualities and are primarily used in jewelry and home décor. Crystals, on the other hand, are naturally occurring or synthetic substances with a crystalline structure. They serve numerous purposes and are frequently used as therapeutic or meditation aids.

Regarding harmonizing the sacral chakra, there is no distinction between stones and crystals. It is a matter of personal preference which method is used to remove blockages and restore energetic balance. Some individuals prefer the appearance of stones, while others find crystals to be more potent. It is ultimately up to you to determine which stone or crystal best suits your requirements.

What Qualities Make a Stone or Crystal Beneficial to the Sacral Chakra?

The sacral chakra is an important energy center located just below the navel in the lower abdomen. This energetic center influences many facets of our existence, including our creativity, sexuality, and pleasure. To support the health of this vital energy center, crystals and stones that resonate with the sacral chakra must be utilized.

In general, it is believed that orange or yellow crystals and stones are particularly beneficial for this chakra. Included among these are carnelian, citrine, and tiger's eye. In addition, any stone or crystal with an earthy or organic quality promotes sacral chakra balance. It is also essential to note that certain crystals, such as quartz and amethyst, must be avoided when working with the sacral chakra.

Understanding what makes a particular stone or crystal effective for our energy centers enables us to make more informed decisions when selecting stones and crystals for healing purposes. Consequently, selecting a stone or crystal that resonates with our sacral chakra enables us to unleash its potential and cultivate greater health and pleasure in all aspects of our lives.

Appearance and Appearance

Orange is associated with the sacral chakra, and many stones and crystals have this hue. However, other colors can also be used to balance the sacral chakra. For instance, red stones are frequently used to stimulate energy and passion, whereas yellow stones encourage imagination and happiness. Typically, any stone or crystal that is visually enticing and has a vibrant color will help to balance the sacral chakra.

When choosing a stone or crystal, it is essential to follow your intuition and select a piece that attracts you. Due to its connection to the emotions, the sacral chakra is an essential energy center to maintain balance. Working with stones and crystals of various hues helps to restore balance to this vital area of the body.

Properties and Development

Numerous practitioners of crystal healing employ stones and crystals with specific properties that align and revitalize this energy center. Different stones and crystals have distinct physical characteristics, such as crystal-forming materials and structures or a pointy, pointed shape.

These properties play an important role in the formation of sacral chakra stones and crystals. Quartz, for instance, is one of the most common materials used in crystal healing due to its powerful vibrations and positive effects on energy transmission. In addition, when held against the skin at this chakra, certain stones, such as red jasper, emanate heat naturally, resulting in feelings of warmth and exhilaration.

Consider the aforementioned properties when selecting a stone or crystal for your sacral chakra, and optimize its strength and alignment with the energies of your body.

Beneficial Stones and Crystals for the Sacral Chakra

Numerous stones and crystals are used to support the health of the sacral chakra, although some are utilized more frequently than others. Below is a list of stones and crystals that are generally considered beneficial for the sacral chakra.

Carnelian Properties: Carnelian is a type of agate whose orange hue is commonly associated with the sacral chakra. In addition to its vibrant hue, the carnelian possesses a number of other qualities that make it an effective sacral chakra balancing crystal. Carnelian, for example, is known to increase creativity, passion, and motivation. In addition to balancing the sacral chakra, this stone improves energy flow and reduces obstructions.

Carnelian is frequently worn as adornment or set in the home or workplace to promote sacral chakra health. For maximum effect, a carnelian is set on or near this energy center during meditation or yoga practice. Carnelian can also be used in crystal healing grids or placed in areas of the home or office where sacral chakra energy needs a boost.

Snowflake Obsidian Properties
Snowflake obsidian is a black igneous material with white patches or patterns that resemble snowflakes. This stone has several advantageous effects on the sacral chakra, including grounding the energy, reducing tension, and promoting tranquility. Snowflake obsidian also aids in the discharge of emotions such as wrath and resentment that obstruct the passage of energy in the sacral chakra.

Snowflake obsidian can be worn as adornment or held during meditation, yoga, or other practices to stimulate the sacral chakra's energy flow. For optimal results, snowflake obsidian should be placed on or near the sacral chakra. This stone is also used in crystal grids and is kept in high-stress or high-tension areas of the home or office.

Citrine is one of the most important stones for the sacral chakra due to its orange hue and association with creativity and prosperity. This stone is renowned for its ability to align the sacral chakra with the lower chakras, allowing energy to flow readily and reducing blockages that cause stagnation. Citrine also enhances creativity, self-confidence, and joy.

To support the sacral chakra, citrine can be worn as jewelry, held during meditation or yoga, or placed in the home or office. In order to induce a sense of calm, this stone can also be added to crystal healing grids or set in areas where anxiety, stress, or tension is prevalent.

Amber is a fossilized tree resin that has been utilized for centuries to promote sacral chakra health. This stone helps regulate the sacral chakra due to its capacity to detoxify and purify energy. In addition, amber is associated with creativity, procreation, and wealth.

Amber can be worn as adornment or placed around the home or office to help cleanse the sacral chakra. Amber should be placed on or near the sacral chakra during meditation or yoga for optimal results. Amber can also be used in crystal healing grids or in areas of the home or office where the energy of the sacral chakra requires a boost.

Different Minerals and Crystals

Numerous additional stones and crystals support the health of the sacral chakra. The list of recommended stones includes amethyst, moonstone, tiger's eye, and garnet. Consult a qualified crystal therapist or energy healer for more information on these and other sacral chakra-supporting crystals and stones.

How to Choose, Cleanse, and Preserve Your Stones and Crystals

A few essential considerations must be taken into account when cleansing and caring for stones and crystals for the sacral chakra. The initial step is to select the appropriate stones or crystals, with a focus on those that resonate most powerfully with the energy of this chakra. Consider orange calcite, carnelian, and tiger's eye as viable alternatives.

Consider the color and clarity of your crystals and stones when caring for them. Ideally, they should appear immaculate and dazzling, with no visible fractures or mineral lines. After selecting your stones or crystals, you must purify them in a basin of cool water overnight or in direct sunlight for a few hours. This will eliminate any negative energies left over from previous proprietors or environments.

Once you are prepared to use stones or crystals for the sacral chakra, you must engage all of your senses while meditating or focusing your energy on this objective. Utilize as many images, sounds, scents, etc. as necessary to feel completely connected and balanced with these therapeutic jewels.

Choosing Your Crystals or Stones

Choose stones that resonate with the energy of the chakra in question. Color is another essential factor to consider. Since this chakra is associated with the color orange, stones in orange or red tones are ideal. In addition, consider other characteristics of crystals and stones, such as how they feel in your hands and which qualities they are believed to enhance. Properly selecting stones can be a potent means of enhancing your spiritual energy and balancing your sacral chakra.

Cleaning Your Crystals or Stones

Regularly cleansing your stones and crystals is one method for maintaining a balanced sacral chakra. It removes any accumulated negativity and allows the stone's positive energy to circulate more freely. There are several methods for cleansing stones.

A few hours of exposure to sunlight is one method. Alternately, purify them with water (by positioning them under flowing water or immersing them overnight in a basin of water) or sound (by striking a bell or chanting near them).

If you are unsure of which method to use, simply grasp the stone in your hand and ask it how it prefers to be cleansed.

Regardless of the method you choose, you must consistently cleanse your stones to maintain the equilibrium of your sacral chakra.

How To Maintain Your Stones Or Crystals

After selecting and cleansing your stones or crystals, you must take proper care of them to preserve their positive energy. Avoid exposing them to abrasive compounds or extreme temperatures, both of which can damage their exterior. Additionally, it is essential to sanitize them frequently, as discussed previously.

In addition to these maintenance instructions, it is recommended to engage in other sacral chakra-related practices. Spending more time in nature, preparing delectable foods, practicing yoga or dance, for example, can increase your creative and sensual activities. Taking care of your stones and crystals and engaging in activities that nourish your sacral chakra maintains the balance and health of this energy center.

Clearly, utilizing crystals and stones is a potent method for enhancing your spiritual energy and balancing your sacral chakra. Numerous stones and crystals are used for this purpose; therefore, you should experiment to determine which ones are most effective.

Look for orange or red-colored stones and crystals that resonate with the energy of the sacral chakra. Additionally, ensure that they are regularly cleansed using one of the aforementioned methods. Remember to regularly care for your stones and engage in activities that nourish your sacral chakra. Using these guidelines when working with crystals and stones will enhance your spiritual energy and restore balance to your sacral chakra.

Chapter 7: Violet

Violet is a lovely hue associated with spirituality and the heavens. Additionally, it is the color of the seventh chakra, the summit chakra. Let us comprehend it better in this chapter.

The Color of Royalty is Violet.

Violet is frequently confused with the color purple, which is truly a combination of red and blue, whereas violet is its own spectral color. Both of these hues are associated with royalty, enlightenment, and paradise.

This color associates melancholy with transformation and letting go of anguish and suffering. It also represents tranquility, profound transformation and transition, and knowledge. It is a color associated with mysticism, purity, cleansing, connection, mysticism, and enchantment.

Violet also represents reconciliation and is recognized as the color that brings people back together and strengthens and mends strained relationships. It is also thought to unite polarities, including not only opposite genders, but also heat and cold, left and right minds, earth and heaven, and night and day.

Balanced use of it allows you to connect well with those around you and the world in which you live. You experience neither duality nor separation; you are one with everything. Obviously, the color of royalty and oneness is the color of the "crown" chakra.

The color violet represents the crown chakra.

The concept of a crown derives from the concept of a corona, which is typically associated with angels and other divine figures. It is believed that enlightened people emit light from their crowns because they have transferred energy upwards through all of their chakras and are now overflowing with light. The seventh chakra is the crown chakra, also known in Sanskrit as 'Sahasrara,' which translates to 'thousand petals.'

Positioned at the summit of your cranium, it is believed that when you activate your crown chakra, you unfurl one petal of wisdom after another and release all of your internalized knowledge, awareness, and wisdom.

On a physical level, it is associated with your cranium, brain, and cerebral cortex, which are responsible for your complete and appropriate functioning and survival. When your crown chakra is activated, you have a healthy nervous system, a keen mind, excellent health and cognition, you feel emotionally, spiritually, mentally, and physically connected to yourself, you have good reflexes, and you are tranquil and energized. It also transforms you into a thoughtful, compassionate, knowledgeable, inquisitive, open-minded, and intellectual individual.

In contrast, amnesia, autism, brain tumor, coma, migraines, and learning disabilities can result from a blocked crown chakra and an imbalance of violet energy in the body.

It can also transform you into a reclusive individual who is unwilling to change or accept new ideas and information. Violet is also associated with idealism, and too much of it can transform you into an idealist who desires the finest of everything.

To maintain a balance of violet energy in your body and to ensure that your crown chakra is functioning properly, utilize violet stones and keep a violet-colored object in your office or living space.

Activating Clairaudience: Hearing Things in Chapter 12

Clairaudience is the ability to hear things that others cannot, and it differs from having a mental disorder with this symptom. With clairaudience, one can perceive entities that exist outside of the physical world. Messages from your guides or ascended masters may originate from the higher dimensions and realms from which you hear them. When you develop a connection with your higher self, you will also be able to receive communications from it whenever you need guidance or are about to engage in an unsafe activity.

How Clairaudience Plays Out

Numerous individuals possess this aptitude but are unaware of it. Because they anticipate something dramatic, such as an actual voice speaking over their shoulder from beside them. Despite the fact that it is possible to hear an actual voice, such as when you are in dire peril and that is the only way to get your attention, clairaudience does not always manifest in this manner. It is more like a very distinct internal voice. It can be more distinct than your typical musings and is most certainly not your voice.

You may have heard your name being called if you've ever experienced clairaudience. Similarly, you may have heard a melody or have a tune trapped in your mind for no apparent reason, typically when you are waking up or going to bed. It is so simple to disregard the tune as merely a tune that gets lodged in your mind. ..However, if you pay close attention to the lyrics, there may be a message for you - not always, but occasionally. When it's a song you don't hear often or haven't heard in a long time, it's important to pay close attention.

When a voice is speaking to you, you have heard that quiet, tiny voice. You know, the one that stops you in your tracks when you're about to do something that will likely land you in hot water? That is the correct item. Occasionally, it may be a random notion that has nothing to do with the train of thought preceding its appearance. Occasionally, it may not be an actual voice, but rather a thought that is so markedly distinct from yours that you can almost perceive it as emanating from a different entity or personality. This invisible personality's aura is typically potent and extraordinary enough to cause you to halt, attend, and pay careful attention.

When you are reading or pondering, clamorous messages sound like your voice. Occasionally, the voice can be heard from the outside as well. If these messages are coming from a benevolent source, they will always feel full of love and light, and they will always be for your highest good. In addition, genuine chloride and messages should not attempt to impose upon your freedom of choice. Your spirit guardians and angels are always willing to offer you advice and direction, but they will not compel you to follow their counsel.

Audience communications can appear as if they are spontaneous thoughts. For instance, you may be making a list of tasks for the day when you have a sudden flashback of your late father throwing you into the air when you were younger. At that moment, your father's spirit may be reaching out to you to say "Hello" because that is a significantly different notion than deciding whether to do the laundry or walk the canines first. This is how sometimes imperceptible clairaudience can be.

You may occasionally receive large downloads or lengthy thoughts and impressions. Have you ever been conversing with someone when you said something so profound and profound that you knew it wasn't actually from you? In fact, one could contend that the message was transmitted to this individual through you. Typically, this missive will contain gold-mine-worthy wisdom. You have a clairaudient experience at these times. Channelers who communicate with their audiences or clients by allowing other entities to converse through them are typically clairaudient and clairsentient as well. They have learned to integrate their energy systems with the intelligent entities with whom they communicate in order to translate the impressions and words they receive into messages that others can comprehend.

Establishing Clairaudience

To develop clairaudience, you must first raise your vibration and activate your chakras, including your third eye. You cannot raise your vibration because the things you will hear have a much higher vibration than the corporeal world. In other words, your frequency must match that of the spiritual dimension in order for you to easily receive communications pertinent to your current circumstance.

Eat Well

To raise your vibration, you must be conscious of the foods you consume. You should consume a great deal of fruits, vegetables, and earth-grown, unprocessed foods. Equally essential is consuming pure, potable water. The more lovingly and respectfully you treat your body, the simpler it will be to access these higher domains of love and light, allowing you to tap into the clairaudient messages sent your way.

•Ask For Help from Your Guides or Higher Self

This can be accomplished by saying a simple prayer affirmation first thing in the morning and last thing at night. You can also accomplish this by meditating with the explicit intent of receiving guidance from your guides. In reality, they are always present and eager to share things with you. Therefore, if you make it apparent that you are willing to listen to them, they will reach out to you and make it simpler for you to communicate with them. Request their assistance in raising your vibration and opening your consciousness so that you remain in alignment with the Divine.

- Practice Silencing Your Inner Voice

Because clairaudient messages typically originate from within, you must learn how to maintain your mind free of all distracting thoughts in order to hear what is being communicated. Your spirits, guides, and other entities will find it difficult to communicate with you if your mind is continuously rushing, bouncing from thought to thought like a chimpanzee leaping through the branches of a tree. It is even more difficult when these notions limit beliefs, doubts, and concerns incessantly. Negative thinking will make it exceedingly difficult for you to receive communications from the other side, unless, of course, other negative beings with nefarious intentions are drawn to you by your low vibratory thoughts. Every day, you should practice mindfulness meditation in order to calm your consciousness. This can be done in conjunction with pranayama techniques.

•Listen to the Sounds Surrounding You

It becomes simpler to give heed to signals from the spirit world when you do this. Because the world we inhabit is extremely chaotic. It is so simple to filter out everything you hear without being aware of doing so. However, these noises can be utilized to your advantage. This is how:

Close your eyes and allow yourself to unwind, wherever you may be.

Set a distinct, resolute intention to enhance your intuitive hearing.

Now listen carefully to the noises around you. Pay close attention, particularly to the tiniest sounds that you typically overlook but are always present.

Continue listening attentively for approximately five minutes, focusing on the quality of each sound.

It is advisable to conduct this exercise in a variety of settings in order to expand your hearing capabilities. Also, observe whether you tend to hear better on your left or right side. You may discover that you hear music better on your left ear and speech better on your right ear, or vice versa.

•Utilize music to enhance your clairaudience

The exercise you are about to read is designed to help you distinguish between the more subtle notes in a song. You will become better at deducing your own thoughts from genuine clairaudient messages the more you practice. Choose music with numerous instrumentals. If you choose to work on a song with few instrumentals, you should pay close attention to the space between each instrument (or line) and the noises.

Put some music on. You can either use speakers or headphones to listen.

Now, concentrate on a particular instrument in the music, such as the percussion, strings, piano, or anything else you can hear.

Isolate this instrument and concentrate on its sonic quality. Observe the feelings it evokes in you.

Switch to a different instrument and focus on it.

This composition can be played repeatedly while focussing on each component.

After focusing on the instruments, you can concentrate on the lyrics and instruments' cadence and rhythm.

When ready, you can concentrate on two instruments simultaneously, concentrating on how they interact. For instance, you can focus on the piano and percussion, then transfer your focus to the piano and strings, etc.

When you feel you have exhausted every aspect of a song to which you can pay attention, pause the music and listen to it internally.

Isolate each instrument in the song in your mind.

In the same manner as in step 7, combine the instruments with the mental hearing.

Now, let the music play in your mind, but with the intention of allowing it to transform into whatever it will.

Instead of attempting to control it, observe how it can remix itself.

Now, adjust the volume of specific instruments while decreasing the volume of others. You can focus on each instrument individually or group them if you prefer.

Experiment with abruptly stopping the music or stopping just one or more instruments simultaneously.

Finally, let the song play in your consciousness and shift your attention from the melody to the actual noises in the room. Alternate between internal hearing and external hearing. This exercise is potent, allowing you to consult your inner wisdom when you're listening to someone and want divine guidance on how to respond to what they're saying or whether they're sincere and trustworthy.

Start actively listening to others. When you make a point of listening to people in order to comprehend what they're saying and what they're not saying, you'll become adept at silencing the portion of your mind that wants to respond rather than pay attention. You will learn to be truly present and to plainly receive what others are communicating, which is excellent preparation for when you begin receiving clairaudient messages from the spirit realm.

•Use Your Imagination

Here is a simple exercise to improve your clairaudience.

Go to a place where you will not be disturbed for at least fifteen minutes.

Ensure that you are wearing comfortable apparel and that all distracting devices are turned off.

Relax your posture and close your eyes.

Take a few deep breaths to attain complete awareness of the present moment. You can use a pranayama technique if you like.

Imagine that you are surrounded by divine creatures who are full of light and love.

Imagine all of your chakras emitting a powerful white light that emanates from you and collides with the light of the other entities, fusing and becoming one.

Feel the expansion of your heart's vitality as your heart connects with these beings and opens up.

Imagine being able to hear the angelic domain. What does it sound like? Do you hear a melody? Do you detect a consistent tone? Don't attempt to imagine how it should sound. Simply permit the sound to reach you. Imagine the sound of a stream if you are having difficulty visualizing what it sounds like. Listen to it gurgling in the forest.

You can also envision ocean waves pounding against the shore or birds tweeting all around you. This exercise seeks to familiarize you with the difference between hearing something internally and receiving it from external influences.

Now, ask these entities if they have anything to impart, and remain silent as you listen. Thank them when they're finished speaking, and carefully emerge from your meditation.

You must remain trusting and receptive throughout this experience, because if you doubt and refuse to follow your intuition and trust your instincts, you may not receive any messages, or your ego-mind may attempt to fill the void with foolishness.

If nothing comes through clearly or you feel uncertain, you can conclude the session with a supplication affirmation to your guides, asking them to help you hear clearly the next time. Do not criticize yourself, and do not feel the need to haste. This process will take some time and a great deal of practice, but eventually you will receive a message from the spiritual sphere that is distinct and unmistakable. Anyone can be clairaudient, so do not feel discouraged. You do not need to be a sorceress or a member of an exclusive society to appreciate the immense benefits of this gift.

The more you choose to act according to your intuition, the more adept you will become at clairaudience. Decide immediately that you will not act without consulting your intuition or your guides, if you are more open to spiritual thinking. When you choose to navigate your daily affairs with spiritual guidance, you will discover that you are significantly better at setting priorities and making the best decisions ever. You will observe that you live with authenticity, clarity, and happiness.

In fact, it is wise to rely on your psychic abilities as much as your physical sensibilities. You have an entire spiritual team of advisors and assistants eager to assist you and provide their perspective. If you dispute this, the next time you encounter a problem, reach out to it in meditation and listen to what it has to say. You would be astonished by the wealth of information and advice that has always been available to you.

Guided Meditation

Guided meditation takes you on a journey to your higher self through the unblocking of your Chakras, allowing positive energy to flow through you. Once your Chakras are balanced and open, you will enjoy a more positive frame of mind. After each guided meditation you will feel free and energized.

Meditation

People who meditate do so for various reasons such as relaxation, improved health, and to balance their Chakras.

Side Effects

Those who are new to meditation or allow themselves to fall deeper into a meditative state than they have been before may experience a few side effects. Some of these side effects may include:

Dizziness

There may be bouts of dizziness or the sensation you are floating. This can occur directly after the meditation or the next day. If you start to feel faint or lightheaded, sit-down and concentrate on your breathing. Close your eyes and take deep even breaths until the feeling passes.

Headaches

Some people experience headaches. Once again take a moment, center yourself, and massage your temples or the base of your skull and neck. Concentrate on your breathing. Breathe in relief and breathe out the pain of the headache. Also, drink a fresh bottle or glass of water. Mint or spearmint tea can also relieve a headache.

Meditation Etiquette and Precautions

As with any discipline, meditation has some etiquette guidelines that must be adhered to. There are also a few precautions a person should take especially as you are reaching for a higher altered state of being.

- Always be respectful of your surroundings, your guides, and the universe.

- Thank your guides, your protectors, and the higher powers that were with you during your meditative journey.

- Never bring any darkness into your light during your meditation.

- Never meditate if you are in a bad place, if you are having a bad day, or are in a bad mood.

- Unless you are in a group session, keep your meditation space private, comfortable, and safe for you.

- Keep electronic devices, except the music system, off and out of your meditation space.

- If you are interrupted during your meditation session do not just drop out of your meditative state. Make sure anyone that may interrupt you knows you need a moment to withdraw from meditation.

- If you suffer from low or high blood pressure, keep medication or a snack, juice, etc. nearby while you are meditating. You may need this if you experience symptoms after your meditation session.

Guided Meditation to Awaken the Throat Chakra

To activate the Throat Chakra, you must establish a connection with your voice and sense the vibrations of your vocal cords. You must carefully consider what you want the universe to hear from you.

Ready Your Environment

You will need thirty to forty-five minutes of uninterrupted time to meditate. Try to choose a place and time that are peaceful and appropriate. If you have a family, a companion, or a roommate, attempt to schedule your study time when no one is at home. Or, inform your roommates that it is now your peaceful time.

Dress comfortably and make sure you are neither too heated nor too chilly. You may choose to wear something blue to enhance your ability to channel the throat chakra's blue energy.

Prepare it beforehand if you have or intend to construct a meditation altar for more intense energy channeling. Have the proper incense or scented colored candle. Friday is an excellent day to meditate in order to stimulate the Throat Chakra.

Make sure the room is adequately illuminated, and if you find it calming and relaxing, play gentle meditation music in the background. Ensure that the room temperature is optimal and that you feel safe and comfortable in your meditation space.

Do not bring or permit anything that will serve as a distraction into the room.

You can recline on the floor with your legs crossed on a mat or blanket. If it's more comfortable for you, you can recline on a cushion on the floor. You may even recline down with your legs crossed or bowed at the knees with your feet securely anchored on the floor if you so choose.

If you are uncomfortable or cannot sit on the floor for some reason, you can rest in a chair with your feet securely planted on the ground. Sitting on the floor or in a chair, it is optimal to meditate barefoot so that your feet are grounded and connected to the earthly sphere.

Guided Meditation for Opening the Throat Chakra

Close your eyes and take a deep, relaxing breath when you are ready to begin. Hold it for two seconds, then release it slowly. Repeat one of the following mantras as you proceed:

Mantra 1: "With this breath, I release the tension, troubles, and upsets of the day."

Mantra 2: "With this breath, I purify my soul and let the world around me fade away."

Mantra 3: "With this breath, I am relaxed, safe, and calm."

Place your hands palm-up in your lap, with the right hand on top of the left. This mudra represents our readiness to receive unadulterated energy from the universe. We are prepared to enter the realm of meditation and explore our subconscious with the aid of the Divine light.

When your hands are in position, inhale and visualize your feet rooting themselves. As you would in the sand, wiggle your toes deeply into the earth to become one with nature. Repeat one of the following mantras as you exhale:

The first mantra is: "With this breath, I become one with nature as I take root."

Mantra 2: "Nature grounds me and I am grateful for her acceptance as I merge with the Great Mother."

Concentrate for a moment on your breathing. Feel its vitality as you inhale and its soothing warmth as you exhale. Become conscious of every cell in your body as you become aware of the rise and fall of your thorax. Inhale once more and feel your breath reaching all the way down to your extremities. Feel your muscles from your toenails to the top of your cranium begin to unwind as you exhale.

Imagine a warm golden radiance beaming in a circle around you. This is the sun or your guardian deity enveloping you in a ring of light and protection. They are there to provide a secure environment while you embark on your ascension.

While basking in their warmth, repeat one of the following mantras:

Mantra 1: "I appreciate the warmth and light. I feel protected, secure, and adored."

Mantra 2: "I am protected, warm, and safe within this circle of light."

Now, you are at ease. Visualize your breath drawing up a blue orb of energy as you take a deep inhalation. Exhale and sense the whirling energy of the orb in front of you. Observe as it transforms into various shades of blue. As the orb of light expands, inhale its energy and allow it to fill you with radiance. Exhale as you expel everything that is holding you back. Allow the blue energy to fill the voids left by your expulsion of negativity.

Repeat softly one of the following mantras as you direct the blue energy to the base of your larynx and sense it resonating with your vocal cords.

First Mantra: "I accept this light and let go of my earthly limitations."

Mantra 2: "I release all thoughts that are holding me back and preventing me from reaching my objectives."

Mantra 3: "I let this pure light in as I become one with the universe; I am the light."

Permit the blue radiance to elevate you. Feel yourself transform into air itself. Let go of anxiety and allow yourself to begin to rise. Feel the blue light's purity permeating you. There is no room for uncertainty here. You are independent, self-assured, and a part of the universe.

Feel the gentle vibrations as the blue energy light flows around and through you.

Allow it to carry you as far as you desire. Allow all thoughts to pass over you as you float, one with the light and the universe. You can allow your thoughts to float away, but you should not obstruct any thoughts or images that may surface. Accept them as they are, process them, and deal with them accordingly. Let inspiration enter you, hear your voice, and let it out. Now is the time to seek guidance or counsel from a higher power by invoking its name.

This is also the time to release any negative thoughts, energies, or tension that have been impeding your energy flow. Now is the time to initiate the healing process so that the blue light can circulate unimpeded through your Throat Chakra.

Feel your breath as you expand your diaphragm with a pure blue energy and light inhalation. As you exhale, feel it purifying your body, mind, and spirit of all the ailments that plague you. Allow your diaphragm to fully decompress for three seconds by exhaling in a slow, constant stream. When you feel completely out of breath, inhale the pristine, spotless blue light. Feel it fill the voids left by your troubles with positivism, assurance, and tranquility.

As you sense your body, mind, and soul being cleansed after a long, difficult day, repeat the following mantra: "With this breath, I purge the toxins that cause me self-doubt, pain, and ill will."

"I breathe in a fresh breath of pure blue light to fill my mind, body, and soul with confidence, courage, and peace."

"I will speak my truth with confidence and expect to be heard."

Relax your respiration and give yourself a few more minutes to meander.

Permitting your thoughts to run their course and your mind to display necessary images. Observe them, recognize them, and then release them. You will know which ones you must follow or pay attention to.

Now, cleanse your mind and refocus your attention on the magnificent blue light. Allow it to tenderly guide you back to earth. Feel yourself return to reality as you inhale the air around you. Watch the light dance around you as you proceed. Thank the light for its healing and guidance.

Immerse yourself once more in the warm golden radiance of your protector. Thank your guardian for keeping you secure throughout the voyage. As the light diminishes, take a deep breath in and as you exhale, release your roots and thank Mother Nature for keeping you grounded.

Focus on your breathing as you gradually open your eyes. Take a moment to observe your immediate environs. Before attempting to stand, inhale deeply and extend your body.

You may experience some dizziness, tingling, or humming. Take a few sips of water and ensure your balance before attempting to walk.

System Of Nutrition And Chakras

Eating is a potent action and one of the ways we take in prana and use it for healing. Consuming sustenance is also one of the most essential activities for our survival and continued existence. Whether you are a nutritionist or not, you are aware that foods facilitate human development, particularly when the proper foods are consumed.

Each chakra has a specific diet that must be followed, and we will discuss each one individually:

Sustenance for the Root Chakra

The root chakra is an ideal location for releasing anxiety associated with sentiments of dishonesty and appetite. Either overeating or undereating may cause disorientation. The function of your root chakra is to help you feel grounded so that you can make wise decisions and interact harmoniously with others.

Minerals, proteins, red foods, medicinal and consumable fungi, and root vegetables are the finest nutritional foods for grounding and enhancing the function of your root chakra.

Eating with other members of your community will also benefit your root chakra. You can also have a conversation with your body in order to respect your body's instinct regarding which of these chakras will restore your chakra the most effectively.

Sustenance for the Sacral Chakra

The sacral chakra opposes the first chakra in every way. While the root chakra grounds and stabilizes us, the sacral chakra allows us to experience movement and fluidity. When you have trouble expressing yourself or being creative, you are not "going with the flow." Eating the proper foods will assist your sacral chakra in maintaining its function.

Seeds, tropical fruits, orange-colored foods, lipids and oils (omega-3s are one of the finest), almonds, and fish are sacral chakra foods.

It is essential to give attention to your senses while consuming.

Dietary Supplements for the Solar Plexus Chakra

The Solar Plexus provides us with the motivation to attain our objectives and make sound decisions. We can also go into acceleration, in which case we will inevitably lose power.

However, you can maximize your strength and vitality by considering the types of foods you consume. Consume foods that will help you maintain your vitality and consume them as frequently as feasible.

Whole cereals, yellow-colored nutritious foods, fiber, legumes, fiber, and complex carbohydrates are among the foods that aid the solar plexus in performing its function.

Avoid foods that will impair your body, such as artificial sweeteners, carbohydrates, and carbonated drinks, and limit your alcohol consumption.

Dietary Supplements for the Heart Chakra

The heart chakra enables us to express affection and compassion. If this chakra is unbalanced, your vital energy will shrivel up.

Foods high in chlorophyll, sprouts, vegetables, any green-colored nutrient-dense food, and raw foods are good for love and compassion.

Additionally, the heart chakra will flourish if you share food with others, express gratitude for nourishing yourself, and infuse love into the water and food we consume during meals.

Nourishment for the Throat Chakra

The pharynx chakra is in charge of illuminating our authenticity and truthfulness. It is also the gateway to our food and the site of several bodily functions, such as digesting, ingesting, inhaling, and speaking.

Fruits, liquids, aquatic plants, sauces, and stews are among the foods that will assist your pharynx chakra in communicating and being truthful.

We should also avoid creating an imbalance in our pharynx chakra, particularly when making food selections; for instance, we should avoid uttering "yes" when we really mean "no"

Dietary Supplements for the Third Eye Chakra

The third eye is the seat of our intuition, inspiration, creativity, and perception. This intuition nourishes our center when we listen to it. If we allow our intellect to supersede our intuition, we risk losing sight.

Herbal tea, blueberries, and blackberries are among the foods that aid our third eye and stimulate our intuitive center.

When your third chakra is unbalanced or in an overdrive state, you should avoid consuming dark chocolate, alcohol, and caffeine. These nutrients will stimulate and maintain your mental and emotional arousal.

Nourishment for Your Crown Chakra

The Crown Chakra is our connection to existence. If you feel disconnected from larger things such as the human race, the planet, your community, or the cosmos, choosing to consume is a highly gratifying form of connection. Eating the proper nutritional foods for the crown chakra will allow you to gain a deeper understanding of the meaning of existence.

Copal, juniper, sage, frankincense, and myrrh are among the foods that support your crown chakra. Also nourish the chakra of your audience with pure air, unconditional love, and moon-and-sun light.

Foods are excellent symbols of connection, allowing you to communicate with the more profound and sacred aspects of existence.

Chakras Immune System and Endocrine System

The endocrine system is a chemical messenger in which internal glands secrete hormones directly into the circulatory system. The internal glands are part of various organs in our bodies, and the endocrine system regulates all of these organs.

All seven Chakras regulate distinct glands:

Root Chakra - regulate adrenal glands

The adrenal glands are located on top of the kidneys and generate hormones, including adrenaline, which stimulates the "flight or fight" response. The adrenaline gland is also responsible for the survival drive of the root chakra, which is directly connected to the base.

Sacral Chakra – regulates the reproductive system, including the ovaries.

The ovaries are in charge of regulating egg production, sexual development, and progesterone and estrogen levels. The energies of the sacral chakra mirror the reproductive potential of the ovaries. Additionally, the sacral chakra is linked to the energies of the genitalia.

Solar Plexus — is in charge of the pancreas

The pancreas produces hormones such as insulin, which aids our digestive systems.

The overstimulation of the solar plexus chakra with substances such as excessive blood sugar can result in a variety of problems that can contribute to diseases such as diabetes. Insufficient stimulation of the solar plexus can result in ulcers.

The Heart Chakra - regulates the Heart and Thymus

The thymus is responsible for the production of lymphocytes, which are vital to digestion and the immune system. Due to this characteristic, the thymus is considered one of the essential restorative properties of the fourth or heart chakra.

Throat Chakra – regulates the thyroid

Both sides of the larynx, which is part of the pharynx chakra, contain the thyroid. The thyroid gland generates the hormone thyroxine, which regulates the rate at which the body converts sustenance into useful energy.

In this region, the pharynx chakra is predominate. The thyroid controls the rate of the metabolic rate.

The Third Eye Regulates the Pituitary Gland

The pituitary gland is located near the base of the cranium and is responsible for releasing hormones that affect the body's composition. The spiritual energies of the third eye are reflected by the pituitary glands and their effect on the entire body.

The pituitary gland and the third eye function together in the organism.

Controlled by the Crown Chakra is the pineal organ

Pineal produces the hormone melatonin and is located deep within the brain.

This hormone reflects the relationship between the crown chakra and other chakras because it influences all of your other endocrine organs.

The crown chakra and pineal gland are part of the system's determining factors.

Other Methods For Caring For The Chakras

Aside from the few things we've discussed in this guide, there are quite a few other techniques you can consider for caring for your chakras and restoring their health. Some of the techniques may not work for you, depending on how your chakras are reacting and what suits your preferences and way of life, but they are all safe, and experimenting with them may disclose unexpected remedies. Among the remedies you can use to care for your chakras are the following:

Meditation

Meditation is one of the first things you should attempt in order to maintain your chakras. This is one of the most popular techniques for repairing the chakras because it is simple and can be incorporated into a variety of aspects of your life. To make this work, you must first locate a comfortable, calm place where you can completely concentrate and keep your mind away from any problems that may be troubling you. Get rid of all distractions, such as sounds, accoutrements, devices, and other items, and contemplate spending time in nature in order to reap the full benefits.

You can choose a specific location that will help you get started with your meditation, or you can choose one that is peaceful and will give you a few moments of serenity before the day begins. Focusing on pleasant, calm, and deep breathing will help you decompress and learn how to release some of the tension within your body.

Innovative ocular technology

This is an excellent one to use if you are coping with tension, which is the primary reason why your chakras are not aligned properly. It is able to alleviate a portion of this tension because it can simulate REM sleep. It will assist you in burying all of your anxiety and concerns deep within your subconscious so that you can concentrate on what is occurring in the present.

Visualization

This technique is similar to meditation, but some people find it simpler because they can concentrate on something other than their steady breathing. This technique is sometimes referred to as creative visualization because you will be able to envision your ideal existence.

With this one, you will be able to attain any ambition you desire by merely visualizing how you would appear, feel, and behave in the future. For instance, suppose you want to be done with education and have a stable position within five years. You would close your eyes and visualize yourself in that time and place. How would your office appear and smell? How would you appear and feel upon achieving your objectives? Often, this will help you feel a bit better and provide you with something to focus on, rather than all the problems and other issues that arise.

Alternately, you can sit alone in a room and imagine a white radiance enveloping you from head to toe, purging you of all the negative energy you've accumulated throughout the day. This negative energy can come from objects, the people around you, and even pollution, so let this white light purge everything. You will begin to feel lighter and so much better about your life with each passing minute.

Crystal therapy

Some individuals choose to maintain their chakras through crystal healing. Do you recall some of the colors and crystals we discussed in a previous chapter? The purpose of crystal healing is to incorporate these into your residence so that you can heal your troublesome chakra. First, you would need to select the crystals and gemstones that would work best for the chakra that you need assistance with, and then you would need to construct a special space in your home.

On a daily basis, or as needed, you would simply recline down and position these crystals on the chakra region you wish to heal. You can also wear these crystals daily, such as with a pendant or a bracelet, and you will begin to observe alterations in your disposition and your body.

Emotional liberation strategy

This is an excellent choice if you wish to practice acupuncture. You would work with a professional who is able to stimulate the chakra-related acupuncture points that may be blocked. Once this is accomplished, all undesirable energy in these points will be expelled. It is beneficial if you have a great deal of pent-up emotions and wish to release them.

Reframing your existing beliefs

We all have certain convictions that we cling to tenaciously and assume will always be correct. However, sometimes it is these beliefs that make it extremely difficult for us to have open and pure chakras. Occasionally, the beliefs are incorrect, or their subject matter is irrelevant to the current situation. If you are concerned that some of your chakras are blocked up and not functioning properly, it may be time to discard some of your outdated beliefs and replace them with ones that will serve you better.

Consume water and stroll around barefoot.

This may not appear to be the most effective method, but it is a good approach to begin communing with the natural world around you. We are actually a part of nature, despite what we may have led ourselves to believe. Therefore, nature is excellent for overcoming our anxieties. Have you ever had a heated argument with someone and then taken a fast drink to calm down? We are reconnecting with nature and incorporating it into our routines.

This is an example of how incorporating nature into our inner lives can benefit us. But our external existence would also benefit from more nature. This is why so many people take the opportunity to go for a walk or spend time outdoors when they are unhappy or just need to get away from the day's problems. Compared to the accoutrements of the modern world, there is something about nature that our bodies and minds adore, as it helps us feel serene and collected.

If you feel that some of your chakras are becoming unbalanced and you need a fast and effective way to bring them back into alignment and feel better, nothing will be as effective as reconnecting with nature. It may be worth your time to remove your shoes and stroll around barefoot for at least a portion of the day.

Self-examination and some introspection

This one may seem a little foreign to you, but it is vital to maintaining your spiritual health and chakras. You must consider yourself your own detective or cleric for this one. It is advisable to ask yourself numerous inquiries. These queries are not intended to make you feel inferior or as if something is wrong with you; rather, they are designed to help you begin to comprehend an extremely vital matter.

These questions are intended to help you understand how your behaviors and activities influence you and whether you alter your behavior based on whether you are alone or with others. If you are aware of these changes and are able to identify them, there may be a few chakras that are out of alignment, and you will need to work to correct them.

The reflection portion will consist of these queries. When you question them, you become genuinely aware of what is happening in your lives and whether or not you need to make adjustments. Be critical, but not harsh, because you want to discover the true answers that will help you align your chakras and feel better.

There are a great number of things you can do to cleanse your chakras and restore their proper functioning. Everyone will discover that a different technique is more effective for them, so don't be disheartened if one doesn't immediately fit into your plan or isn't functioning well for you. Just play around with them a bit and work your way down the list, and you will definitely discover the ideal one for you!

The Sources Of Chakra Information

The origin of chakras can be traced back to primordial Hindu culture. Consequently, it has strong connections to the various practices, rituals, and traditions that are associated with Hinduism. It has a significant impact on yoga. Let's examine the various sources from which we've gained knowledge about the chakras.

Information Compilation

The Upanishads have been used to compile the information that is currently available to us. The Upanishads constitute the entirety of Hinduism's sacrosanct writings, which have been compiled from various Hindu scriptures. These sacred texts are written in Sanskrit and are known as the Vedas. The four Vedas are the Rig Veda, the Sama Veda, the Yajur Veda, and the Atharva Veda. The Upanishads are the Vedas' subscripts. In Sanskrit, the term Veda literally translates to "knowledge." It is impossible to pinpoint a specific date for when the Vedas were written or compiled, as they date back so far into antiquity. As early as the seventh century, the earliest Upanishads were discovered. There are 108 Upanishads in total, and 13 of these Upanishads contain essential information about Chakras. Upanishad's literal translation in Sanskrit is "those who sit nearby." Oral transmission was the means by which ancient doctrines were passed down through the generations. Consequently, it is believed that a person who can attend to the principles attentively will be incapable of applying them in practice.

Origins of Chakras

Not only is there more than one interpretation of the meaning and perception of chakras, but also of their functions. Chakras have become a common term used in ordinary conversations, and they no longer have a foreign or exotic ring to them. In the past decade or so, yoga and all of its associated concepts have acquired a tremendous amount of popularity. In tandem with the rise in yoga awareness, there appears to be an increase in the confusion surrounding these concepts. Existing contradictory viewpoints, misguided opinions, and inaccurate information have only exacerbated an already chaotic situation. And as a result, people's perceptions of chakras and attitudes towards them have increased dramatically. If you truly desire to conquer your control over the chakras, you must have a comprehensive and distinct understanding of chakras and all related concepts. Chakras have been around for more than a few hundred years and are a part of the primordial rituals and traditions that have been handed down through the generations. And this is perhaps one of the most common aspects of yoga that most modern instructors of this ancient art seem to neglect, as they have also failed to explore this esoteric field in depth.

While keeping all of this in mind, it is crucial that you comprehend their origin and history. Therefore, let us examine their history. But before we delve into learning about the chakras, let's briefly review the Vedas. The Vedas are the ancient Hindu scriptures from India, dating back to between 1500 and 500 B.C. These scriptures are exhaustively documented documents on a variety of topics. These documents were originally written in Sanskrit and are considered the earliest known record of not only literature written in Sanskrit but also Hindu scriptures. It is reasonable to consider that the Vedas also represent an ancient tradition, the tradition of transmitting the Brahmins' oral recitals from generation to generation. Next, you will need to understand what a Brahmin is. A Brahmin is a Hindu who has atoned with the divine and the cosmos.

Chakra is a Sanskrit word, and its literal meaning is "wheel." In this context, "wheel" refers to the wheels that are attached to monarchs' chariots. In ancient India, rulers were known as Chakravartin, which can also be used as an allegory for the Sun. Popular belief holds that the Sun has the ability to transcend all terrestrial boundaries. The term chakra is also associated with the wheel of time, or kalachakra. The kalachakra is eternal and represents not only the harmony necessary for a better existence, but also the divine order. In conclusion, the kalachakra are associated with the chakras and have the ability to transcend all mortal boundaries and provide the Universe with the balance that it requires.

The two approaches that can be taken to comprehend the concept of chakras could not be more dissimilar from one another. We will examine both of these approaches. The first approach has connections to the human realm, while the second has ties to the divine. Let's examine the first strategy in more detail. According to prevalent belief, the advent of a new sovereign would herald in the beginning of a new era. And if you examine all the descriptions of the rulers, you will observe that it was said that each of these men had a disk of illuminated golden light around his head, similar to the halo of Christ. This halo can be viewed as a representation of their extraordinarily vibrant third chakra.

Now, let's examine the second strategy. The second strategy derives from Hindu mythology. It was believed that when Lord Vishnu descended to Earth, each of his four limbs contained a distinct object. These items included a lotus blossom, a bivalve, a club, and a chakra. These are the two historical and mythological approaches to understanding the concept of chakras.

Vedas are the ancient Indian scriptures that are associated with Hinduism. Originally, Sanskrit was the language used to compose these scriptures. Upanishads follow. The Vedas are the genus, while the Upanishads are the species. The Upanishads contain all of the doctrines that have been transmitted from instructors to disciples. Yoga and Patanjali's yoga sutras are the Upanishads that contain references to chakras and describe how chakras are believed to be the consciousness vortices of the body. In the Patanjali sutra, the eightfold path, which is part of the classic yoga tradition, is explained in great detail.

This sutra was initially very dualistic in nature. This sutra emphasized that nature and spirit were distinct entities, not a single entity. This sutra outlines the path to enlightenment, which includes certain austere practices and the renunciation of one's fundamental essence. Chakras and Kundalini became an indisputable component of yoga only after the adoption of Tantra, a non-dualist tradition by nature. In India, numerous spiritual traditions have existed since antiquity, and the teachings of Tantra have evolved from the synthesis of these various traditions. Only between the sixth and seventh centuries A.D. In the seventh century A.D., these teachings gained popularity. Prior to this, the dualistic perspective was prevalent.

The dualistic and non-dualistic theories are polar opposites, as you may have deduced from their respective names. The non-dualistic theory held that everything was a component of a unique entity and that the sum of all its parts comprised the whole. Tantra's perception in the West appears to be based on a clear misunderstanding of the concept. It is believed that Tantra is a carnal tradition. Yes, sexuality is an undeniable aspect of Tantra, but Tantra is not exclusively concerned with sexuality. Tantric traditions revere sexuality as holy. Because of this, the body is regarded as a sacred sanctuary, and it is believed that our consciousness resides within it. However, this is only a minor portion of the Tantra theory. Tantra is all about weaving together various Kundalini and hatha yoga-related principles. There are numerous components that comprise Tantra, and each is accorded equal importance.

Let's examine the literal definition of the word Tantra. Tantra means loom, and this represents the tantric tradition, which is all about interweaving the various threads to create the tapestry of unity. Nature consists of opposing forces, and true unity can only be attained when these forces are in perfect harmony. This is the foundation of the chakra system, which can be viewed as a branch of tantra.

There are many opposing forces in nature, which can be thought of as yin and yang, such as spirit and matter, body and mind, masculine and feminine, etc. All of these may appear to be entirely distinct, but they must be combined in order to achieve harmony, as is recorded in the Vedas. As far back as the tenth century, there exists a wealth of information on chakra meditation. Texts such as Satkaranirupana, Padakapancaka, and Gorakshashatakam provide crucial information about the chakras and serve as the cornerstones for all chakra-related knowledge available today.

Existence of a subtle body and the seven chakras, which interact with the physical body, is a feature shared by all traditions and philosophies associated with the world's current philosophies. And now it is imperative that you gain a deeper comprehension of the concept of subtle body. This concept can be comprehended simply as follows.

The subtle body can be conceived of as a psychic framework that is superimposed on our physical body. The subtle body is present in all living things and can be measured as electromagnetic energy fields. This implies that the subtle body exists not only in living organisms but also in plants and animals. According to yoga traditions, the subtle body is comprised of five distinct strata, each of which has a different degree of refinement and is referred to as a Kosha. If you examine the center of your body, you will perceive the subtle body to be a chakra at this juncture. There are seven of these main chakras in the human body, and they are responsible for generating the aura fields of a person.

The origin of a person's aura would be the point at which the patterns generated by the various chakras interact with the various forces of the external universe. The location of the chakras within the human body is one of the most frequently made observations. It is intriguing to note that the chakras are present along the entire length of the spinal column and are located in close proximity to the vital organs of the human body. There are a number of minor chakras that contribute to our well-being in addition to the primary chakras. The first chakra is known as the soma chakra and is located above the third eye, while the second secondary chakra is located near the heart chakra. These were the two most significant subordinate chakras. According to other systems, however, the number of chakras in the body varies. Some contemplate nine, while others may consider twelve or seven. This number is debatable, and rightly so, because a chakra is regarded as the center of our energy and consciousness, and there are consequently no restrictions on the number of chakras present.

According to the original chakra system, there are only seven chakras, and these seven chakras have influence over the seven vital organs of the human body. Moreover, mastering control over these seven chakras is a challenging endeavor that could take a lifetime to achieve. It is not a simple undertaking at all, as there are numerous ways to interpret the chakras that exist in our world. And according to some of these interpretations, the higher chakras are more important than the lower ones. During a period in our history when mind over matter was emphasized by the majority of the world's main religions, this viewpoint emerged. From this arose the hypotheses that helped deny the very existence of a spiritual element in the material universe. When you pay attention and attentively read the tantra-related text, you will realize that the higher chakras have never been favored. In fact, the opposite is stated: for a person to achieve atonement, he or she must pass through all the phases of these chakras, and only by integrating them into a single being can they achieve atonement. The lower chakras provide the necessary basis for the existence of the higher chakras.

Subtle frame

Every being possesses a subtle body, and it is not a construct of mythology; it actually exists. All seven of the body's main chakras are located within the subtle body. If you truly wish to gain a deeper comprehension of chakras and related concepts, you must first comprehend the meaning of subtle body. Spirituality is not an exact discipline, and there are no absolute principles, so there is room for individual interpretation. This is one of the primary reasons why attempting to define subliminal body is extremely difficult. The earliest mention of subtle body dates back to 500 B.C. and can be found in a Hinduism and spirituality-related text. In addition to this particular Upanishad, numerous other Upanishads also describe this abstract concept.

Due to the fact that subtle body in Sanskrit is sukshma sharira, it is exceedingly difficult and perplexing to convey the meaning of this concept. The literal translation of sukshma in Sanskrit is "subtle and minute, sometimes dark or even empty." Additionally, the same term can be used to describe a person's mental state. The meaning of this word varies depending on how it is used and the surrounding context. And because of this, it is extremely difficult to have a precise and fixed meaning, making its literal translation a formidable challenge. Let us now proceed on to the phrase's second word. Moreover, it is sharira. The literal meaning of the word sharira is "body," but depending on the context and usage, it can also mean "husk" or "frame." When a single word has multiple meanings depending on the context in which it is used, it becomes very difficult to define it.

Visualize sukshma sharira as a complex network of channels through which prana can flow for the simplest understanding of this concept. These cannot be considered individual channels because they lack their own essence. According to Hinduism, prana refers to the life force and is regarded as the ultimate manifestation of existence as a whole.

Let us now summarize the concept of sukshma sharira, also known as subtle body. Subtle body can be thought of as the immaterial or psychic presence responsible for linking and connecting our consciousness and physical body. The sukshma sharira facilitates the interaction between the physical and immaterial forms. Numerous attempts have been made to elucidate the concept of subtle body, despite its extreme difficulty. This concept is difficult to express due to the varying ways in which it is perceived, as well as the fact that it has multiple interpretations. But the main reason this concept is difficult to define is that it is impossible to explain the existence of something that cannot even be seen with the unaided eye.

Let's put all of these difficulties aside. It is crucial that you comprehend the idea of subtle body. Because the chakras are present within this dimension. The human body contains seven major chakras, and the location of these seven major chakras corresponds precisely with the seven major nerves that emerge from the vertebral column. In addition to these seven main chakras, there are additional secondary chakras, and more information about them will be provided in the following chapters.

Improving Your Chakra System

The remainder of this book will focus on specific areas of alternative therapy and how they can assist you in balancing your sacral chakra. But you can also regain balance by making modifications to your general way of life.

Our contemporary way of life can wreak havoc on the chakra system. We spend so much time indoors, shut off from the natural world, that sometimes we don't even breathe natural fresh air for days, moving from the home, to the car, to the office, or some other 'inside' location to spend the working hours.

We have lost our connection with the natural world, often being unaware of the phase of the moon at night or the origin of our food outside of the supermarket. The majority of us have lost touch with natural food, purchasing and consuming processed, pre-packaged, and takeout dishes that often do not even resemble food.

Even information and entertainment can be detrimental to our energy field.

The television, movies, and social media are filled with negative messages, including violence, wrath, conflicts, agony, peril, avarice, out-of-control self-interest, and human disaster. All of them exemplify extremely negative energy, which is their only shared characteristic.

These are the types of issues that can obstruct the sacral chakra and lead to difficulties in life; however, how can you alter this?

Taking the time to 'smell the flowers' can have a profound effect on your energy field.

Spend time outdoors, where you can breathe actual oxygen and wander on the earth as opposed to concrete. Spend no time jogging, cycling, or participating in vigorous sports. All of that may be beneficial for your physical health, but you also need leisurely time, time spent meandering in a garden or park, time spent wandering in the country or along the coast, and time spent observing the work you've put into your garden.

Taking the time to breathe real, pure air and making time for yourself in your life is not at all egotistical. We have been conditioned to believe that taking time for oneself is the worst form of selfishness, particularly but not exclusively for women. We are accustomed to putting everyone and everything ahead of our own requirements, but taking time for yourself is the antithesis of selfishness.

When you allow yourself time to recuperate, calibrate your energy field, and unwind, you will be better able to interact with others and accomplish more in less time and with less effort.

We are a part of nature, and being in nature nourishes our energy field, so try going for a walk in a park or in the countryside, where you can smell the fragrance of nature, observe the color of the blossoms, and feel the texture of the trees. A stroll on the shore can fill your lungs with delightful fresh air, and walking barefoot on the sand is both a unique experience and a great exfoliator for your feet.

Being conscious of the seasons, the phases of the moon, and the ancient festivals of nature is a marvelous way to reconnect with the earth's natural energy and our own natural energy.

If you have access to a garden or outdoor space, you should utilize it. Growing flowers can add elegance to your life, while growing your own herbs and vegetables can not only provide you with fresh air and exercise, but also provide you with fresh, organic ingredients for cooking. There is nothing more delicious than a freshly harvested salad from your garden, balcony, or windowbox.

You should also work to develop and strengthen your relationships with others. Our personal lives can become extremely limited and lonely. Numerous individuals reside alone or in a series of brief relationships. Even when we are part of a positive relationship or a loving family, it is not uncommon for us to not even know our next-door neighbors, to live in an area with no ties to the surrounding community, and to treat our residence as a dormitory rather than a home. This feeling of social isolation can harm the energy of the sacral chakra and, over time, deplete your essential energy.

Make an effort to communicate with others. Join organizations, socialize locally, become involved in your local church, or join a club.

A healthy energy field and chakra system requires a sense of belonging and sharing, as well as a connection to and willingness to aid others.

The sacral chakra and hormonal balance

We frequently discuss hormones, particularly female hormones, without a clear comprehension of what they are and how they affect the entire system.

Hormones are produced throughout the body by glands. They are chemical mediators that travel through the circulation and penetrate tissues, where they regulate growth, emotions, reproduction, and metabolism, as well as overall health and well-being.

A deficiency in insulin causes diabetes, a deficiency in oestrogen can cause weight gain or heat flushes, and recent research confirms that an excess of testosterone can be the cause of increased aggression in some males.

Hormones are highly potent. It only takes a small quantity to induce life-altering alterations in cells or the entire organism. This is why excess or deficiency of a particular hormone can be dangerous. If you have symptoms of a hormone disorder, your physician can arrange for laboratory tests to measure the hormone levels in your blood, urine, or saliva.

Similar to professional pregnancy tests, home pregnancy tests detect pregnancy hormones in urine.

In conclusion, regulated hormones are essential for a healthy system.

Each of the seven main chakras affects various glandular systems. Therefore, maintaining a balanced chakra system will automatically have a balancing effect on your hormone system.

In most cases, the chakra corresponds to a specific gland in the endocrine system; however, there is some disagreement regarding the glands associated with the sacral root chakra.

Some people assert that the adrenal glands and sacral chakra are connected, which makes sense because they are the most physically interconnected organs in the body.

However, another school of thought asserts that the gonads - the ovaries and testes - have an affinity for the sacral chakra due to the physical effects of the hormones they produce. My own experience working with the chakras, as well as the fact that the sacral chakra is most clearly linked to our sexuality, lead me to subscribe to this particular school of thought.

Ovaries and Testes
The gonads are the sex organs and are therefore involved in a balanced sexuality, the reproductive system, and reproduction, but they are also more complex than that.

These glands produce the hormones that regulate body hair, voice volume, and reproduction, among other things.

The ovaries (female) produce the female hormones Progesterone and Oestrogen. They contribute to the health of reproductive tissues, breasts, epidermis, and the brain. Cancer can result from excessive stimulation of the breasts, ovaries, and uterus. Excess estrogen can cause fluid retention, weight gain, migraines, and, more severely, overstimulation of the breasts, ovaries, and uterus.

Many menopausal symptoms, such as heat flashes, vaginal dryness, accelerated skin aging, and excessive bone loss, can be caused by insufficient estrogen. dementia has also been linked to it.

In males, excess oestrogen relative to testosterone is believed to cause prostate issues.

The testes (male) produce male reproductive hormones, primarily testosterone, which affects the growth of muscle mass and strength, as well as enhanced bone density, growth, and strength. It is also the hormone responsible for the deepening of the voice and the growth of the beard.

www.ingramcontent.com/pod-product-compliance
Lightning Source LLC
Chambersburg PA
CBHW050250120526
44590CB00016B/2289